Explore!
TUDORS

Jane Bingham

D0314544

First published in 2015 by Wayland

Copyright © Wayland 2015

Wayland
338 Euston Road
London NW1 3BH

Wayland Australia
Level 17/207 Kent Street
Sydney, NSW 2000

 Produced for Wayland by
White-Thomson Publishing
www.wtpub.co.uk
+44 (0)843 208 7460

All rights reserved

Editor: Jane Bingham
Designer: Tim Mayer
Picture researcher: Jane Bingham
Illustrations for step-by-step: Stefan Chabluk
Proof reader: Lucy Ross

A cataloguing record for this title is available
from the British Library.

ISBN 978 0 7502 8880 4

Dewey Number 942'.05-dc23

10 9 8 7 6 5 4 3 2 1

Printed in China

Wayland is a division of Hachette Children's
BRENT LIBRARIES company

www.hachette.co.uk

BRENT LIBRARIES	
91120000214406	
Askews & Holts	09-Jan-2015
J942.05	£8.99

Picture acknowledgements:
The author and publisher would like to thank the
following agencies and people for allowing these
pictures to be reproduced:

Cover (top left) Wikimedia; (top right)
BrendanHunter/iStock; (sign background)
Andrey_Kuzmin/Shutterstock (bottom left) Jane
Rix/Shutterstock; (bottom right) Wikimedia;
p.1 (left) Wikimedia; (right) Wikimedia; p.3 Cenap
refik ongan/Shutterstock; p.4 Wikimedia; p.5
(top) Georgios Kollidas/Dreamstime; (bottom)
Wikimedia; p.6 Wikimedia; p.7 Wikimedia; p.8
Wikimedia; p.9 Wikimedia; p.10 Bridgetjones/
Dreamstime; p.11 Wikimedia; p.12 Fotomolos/
Dreamstime; p.13 (top) Sergiy Artsaba/
Shutterstock; (bottom) MoreenBlackthorne/
Shutterstock; p.16 Angelina Dimitrova/
Shutterstock; p.17 (top) Look and Learn/
Bridgeman Art Library; (bottom) Jef Thompson/
Shutterstock; p.18 Mrsmas/Dreamstime; p.19
(top) Neftali/Shutterstock; (bottom) Mary
Evans Picture Library/TAH Collection; p.20
Laszlo Szirtesi/Shutterstock; p.21(top) Daniel
Gale/Shutterstock; (bottom) Wikimedia; p.22
LubaShi/Shutterstock; p.23 (top) Jiawangkun/
Dreamstime; (bottom left) homydesign/
Shutterstock; (bottom right) Wikimedia; p.24
Wikimedia; p.25 (top) Library of Congress;
(bottom) Wikimedia; p.26 (top) Wikimedia;
(bottom) Wikimedia; p.27 (top) Cenap refik
ongan/Shutterstock; (bottom) Padmayogini/
Shutterstock; p.28 Wikimedia; p.29 (top
left) Tonybaggett/Dreamstime; (top right)
Wolna/Shutterstock; (bottom) Diana Talium/
Shutterstock; p.32 Mrsmas/Dreamstime.

Please note:
The website addresses (URLs) included in this book were
valid at the time of going to press. However, because of the
nature of the Internet, it is possible that some addresses
may have changed, or sites may have changed or closed
down since publication. While the author and publishers
regret any inconvenience this may cause to the readers,
no responsibility for any such changes can be accepted by
either the author or the publishers.

Contents

Who were the Tudors?

The Tudors were a family of kings and queens who ruled England from 1485 to 1603. They gave their name to a famous period in English history. Later, the term 'Tudors' came to have a wider meaning, covering all the men, women and children living in England at the time.

Tudor monarchs

Five Tudor monarchs ruled England. Henry VII was the first, followed by his son, Henry VIII. After the death of Henry VIII, each of his three children ruled in turn. When Queen Elizabeth died, the Tudor period came to an end.

This painting shows King Henry VIII and his children. Edward, Mary and Elizabeth are pictured as they looked when they ruled England.

Exciting times

Trading flourished and towns grew rapidly in the 16th century. Tudor monarchs encouraged artists, writers and musicians. Daring explorers reached new lands and the English Navy was respected and feared. By the 1600s, England had become a rich and powerful nation.

William Shakespeare was one of many brilliant writers working in the Tudor period.

Tudor people

Wealthy families lived in luxury. They owned enormous mansions and held lavish feasts. Meanwhile, life was very hard for the poor. There was not enough work for everyone and the city streets were filled with beggars.

Some clever traders became immensely rich. This portrait shows a merchant dressed in fine clothes.

5

Two powerful kings

King Henry VII came to the throne in 1485 after a violent struggle for power. During his reign he gained control of the English nobles, encouraged merchants and traders, and built up a fortune for the crown. When he died in 1509 he left a well-run kingdom to his son.

Henry VII is often known as Henry Tudor. He brought peace and order to England, but he was not greatly loved by his people.

A new young king

The young King Henry VIII was a very popular ruler. He was handsome and lively and loved music, dancing and sport. Henry married Catherine of Aragon, a Spanish princess, and they had a daughter, Mary. However Catherine did not produce a son to inherit the crown.

Henry and the Church

When he was in his thirties, Henry fell in love with Anne Boleyn, a young woman at court. He decided that he must divorce Catherine and marry Anne. At that time, divorces were granted by the Pope in Rome, and the Pope refused to allow it. Henry realised that he would have to break away from the Roman Catholic Church. In 1531 Parliament declared him head of the Church in England.

Many wives

Anne Boleyn had a daughter, called Elizabeth, leaving Henry still desperate for a son. After just three years of marriage, Anne was executed and Henry married Jane Seymour. Henry was delighted when Jane gave birth to Edward, but sadly she died soon afterwards. Henry went on to marry three more times. His next two wives were Anne of Cleves, a German princess, and Catherine Howard, an English noblewoman. Neither of these marriages lasted long. Anne was sent to live in the country and Catherine was beheaded. Henry's last wife, Catherine Parr, looked after him until his death at the age of 55.

Edward, Mary and Elizabeth

In 1547, the nine-year-old son of Henry VIII became King Edward VI, but he never had the chance to rule alone. Edward Seymour, the young king's powerful uncle, governed England on his behalf until his death at the age of 15.

Mary Tudor

After Edward's death in 1553, his older sister Mary was crowned queen. She was the oldest daughter of King Henry VIII and she is often known as Mary Tudor. Mary had been brought up as a Roman Catholic and she hated the Protestant Church of England. During her five-year reign, over 300 people were burned at the stake because they belonged to the Church of England.

Mary Tudor was given the nickname 'Bloody Mary' because she gave orders for so many people to be put to death.

Queen Elizabeth

Elizabeth reigned for over 50 years, from 1558 to 1603. She chose experienced advisers to help her govern wisely, and stayed single all her life, saying she was married to England. Even though she was head of the Church of England, she did not persecute Roman Catholics.

This painting of Elizabeth is known as the Armada portrait. The two background scenes show the defeat of the Spanish Armada.

A glorious victory

In 1588, England faced great danger. King Philip II of Spain sent a large fleet of ships, called the Spanish Armada, to invade England. Fortunately, the English were well prepared and their warships scattered the Spanish fleet. It was a glorious victory for Elizabeth, and her people named her Gloriana.

A brilliant court

Elizabeth invited poets, musicians and playwrights to perform for her, and welcomed explorers to her court. When she died, at the age of 69, she was succeeded by James I, the first of the Stuart monarchs.

Rich and poor

Charlecote Park in Warwickshire was built in 1558. Tudor palaces were surrounded by beautiful gardens.

Tudor England was a place of great contrasts. Nobles and wealthy merchants lived in enormous mansions and enjoyed many luxuries. Poor families had small, tumbledown homes and often went hungry.

Different homes

Noble families lived in palaces and manor houses built from timber, brick and stone. Some palaces had more than 100 bedrooms, and were run by a large staff of servants. Poorer homes were usually made from wood and plaster. Families were often crowded into a single room and it was not unusual for a whole family to share the same bed.

This painting of a London feast shows the costumes of both rich and poor.

Different clothes

The rich wore elaborate clothes made from silk and velvet, covered with jewels and embroidery. Men wore fitted jackets, known as doublets, padded trousers, called breeches, and tights, called hose. Women often wore low-cut dresses with wide skirts supported by hoops. Poor people were forbidden by law from wearing colourful clothes. Their clothes were made from wool or linen and coloured with natural dyes.

Different diets

Rich people ate three meals a day. Their main meal was served around 11 in the morning. It included a lot of meat and fish, which had been preserved by salting or smoking. For breakfast and supper, they had bread, beef and beer. Poor people survived mainly on bread and porridge. If they lived in the country they ate vegetables, eggs and small amounts of meat.

A kitchen maid's day

Tudor servants had to work extremely hard. This imaginary diary entry describes a day in the life of a young kitchen maid.

I wake up early at five o'clock and start work straightaway. My first job is to stoke the kitchen fire. Then I go out to the courtyard and fill six buckets of water from the well.

Today, my master and mistress are holding a feast so I have many jobs to do. I am in charge of roasting a wild boar on a spit. I have to turn the spit handle very slowly so every part of the boar gets cooked.

When I'm not busy turning the spit, I chop up vegetables and prepare the herbs and spices for the sauces. I grate a little nutmeg, and use a pestle and mortar to grind up cinnamon and cloves.

At midday my mistress comes to check on our work. She inspects all the pies and puddings and tastes the sauces. She tells me she is pleased with me, and soon I will be able to serve at table!

The feast begins at three o'clock and lasts for many hours. Everything goes well, but I'm kept very busy cleaning pots and pans. It is midnight before I finish and then I have to scrub the kitchen table clean. By the time all my work is done, I hardly have the strength to climb up the stairs to my bed in the attic!

The diary entry on this page has been written for this book. Can you create your own diary entry for a boy or girl who lives in a Tudor town and helps out in the family workshop? Use the facts in this book and in other sources to help you write about a day in their life.

Make Tudor gingerbread

Tudor gingerbread was made from breadcrumbs flavoured with ginger and other spices. It was not as crunchy as our modern gingerbread biscuits and it was often coloured red and decorated with herbs. Why not try this simple recipe for Tudor-style gingerbread?

Ingredients

6 tablespoons of clear honey

6 slices slightly stale white bread, with the crusts cut off

2 teaspoons ground ginger

2 teaspoons ground cinnamon

$^1/_2$ teaspoon ground black pepper

Red food colouring (optional)

Small herb leaves to decorate

1

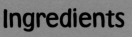

Use your fingertips to crumble the bread into breadcrumbs in a large mixing bowl. Then add the ginger, cinnamon and pepper.

2

Warm the honey until it is quite runny. (You can do this carefully in a saucepan.) Pour the honey into the bowl with the breadcrumbs and spices.

3

Stir the mixture. If it is too runny, add more breadcrumbs. Then add a drop or two of red food colouring.

4

Line a shallow rectangular cake tin with non-stick paper. Press the mixture into the tin, making sure the top is level. Leave the tin in the refrigerator for an hour or two, until the mixture is firm.

5

Turn the gingerbread block onto a clean chopping board and cut it into small squares. Decorate the squares with herb leaves and offer them to your friends!

Tudor towns

Towns grew rapidly in the 1500s. Around 6000 people arrived in London each year, and Bristol and Norwich also expanded fast. Tudor towns were noisy, smelly and crowded, but there were quieter areas where wealthy citizens lived.

Busy streets

The city streets were lined with shops and workshops. Butchers, bakers and brewers set up permanent shops, while fruit, milk and cheese were sold in markets. Workshops were open at the front so customers could see the craftsmen at work. In the larger cities, each trade had a different street, so people knew where to find all the tailors, potters or leatherworkers.

This model shows a small Tudor town on a snowy winter night. The houses were built very close together.

People of all classes met on the streets.

Dirt and disease

Tudor towns were unhealthy places. Animals roamed freely and food was left to rot on the streets. There were no proper drains and few homes had toilets, so chamber pots were simply emptied out of windows. In these unhealthy conditions, disease spread rapidly and the young, weak and old were the first to die.

Crime and punishment

Violence and crime flourished in the towns. Thieves roamed the streets and fights broke out in taverns. There was no police force to keep the peace, but people who broke the law faced harsh punishments. Minor criminals were locked in the stocks. Those who had committed serious crimes were usually sentenced to death. They were hung in public on a gallows.

Crowds gathered around the stocks to laugh at wrongdoers. They threw rotten food at the prisoners and called them names.

17

Fun and games

Most people in Tudor times managed to have some fun. They could visit their local fair, watch a tournament or see a play at the theatre. Skittles and bowls were very popular and some wealthy gentlemen played an early form of tennis.

Tournaments

Kings and noblemen took part in tournaments. They dressed in suits of armour and charged at each other with lances. Wealthy spectators watched the show from tent-like buildings called pavilions. Poorer people gathered around the tournament ground.

A modern reconstruction of a tournament

Theatres

People of all classes enjoyed a trip to the theatre. Poor people stood in the yard in front of the stage, while richer people had seats. Tudor audiences were not very well-behaved. If people did not like a play, they booed loudly!

This postage stamp shows the Rose Theatre beside the River Thames.

An artist's impression of a Tudor fair

All the fun of the fair

Tudor fairs were places to buy and sell goods and to hire workers. But people also went to the fair to enjoy themselves. Musicians and acrobats performed for the crowds, and young men joined in wrestling matches and tugs-of-war. Other entertainments included bear-baiting and cock-fighting. The Tudors were not shocked by shows that involved cruelty to animals.

Exploring the world

The Tudor period was a very exciting time for explorers. After Christopher Columbus reached America in 1492, sailors dreamt of finding fabulous riches in the New World. They also hoped to discover new trading routes to India and China.

Tudor explorers crossed the oceans in small, wooden ships. This is a modern copy of the *Golden Hind*, in which Sir Francis Drake sailed around the world.

In search of new routes

In 1497, John Cabot sailed west from Bristol in search of a route to Asia. He reached Newfoundland, which he believed was Asia, and claimed it for England. Almost 80 years later, Martin Frobisher sailed up the northeast coast of Canada. He believed he had found a route to the East. In fact, he had arrived in a large bay.

Around the world

Sir Francis Drake was a brilliant sea captain, but he was also a raider and a pirate. He spent most of his career attacking and looting Spanish ships. Between 1577 and 1580 he sailed around the world, raiding as he went. When he returned to England he was knighted by Queen Elizabeth.

Making maps

As sailors gained more knowledge of the world, there were great advances in map-making. Henry VIII employed a team of map-makers at Greenwich. One of these was Sebastian Cabot, son of the explorer John Cabot. King Henry paid him to map the coasts of Brazil and the West Indies.

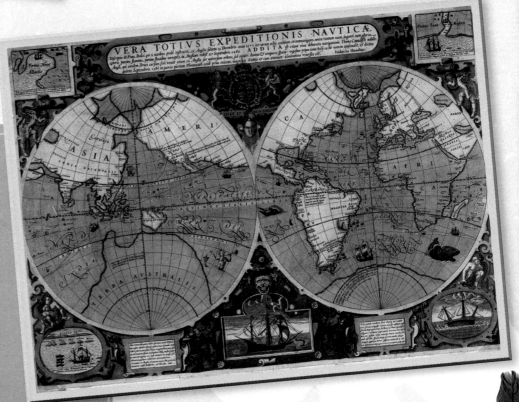

This English map of the world was made in 1595. The continent of Europe is shown in detail, but the outlines of North and South America are not very accurate.

Traders and settlers

By the start of the Tudor age, English merchants were buying goods from India, North Africa and the islands of Southeast Asia. They imported a range of valuable products, such as spices, cotton and silk, but most of these goods reached Europe through the ports of Venice and Constantinople (now called Istanbul). Merchants had to pay very high prices and were keen to make their own trading deals.

The Tudors imported cinnamon, nutmeg and cloves to use for cooking and making medicines.

Trading deals

By the 1590s, English trading ships were sailing directly to Africa and Asia, and in 1600 a group of merchant seamen established the East India Trading Company. English merchants also made deals in Russia and Japan and with the Turks of the Ottoman Empire.

Settlers in America

In 1585, Sir Walter Raleigh sent five ships to North America with the aim of forming an English colony. The settlers made their base on Roanoke Island (now in the state of North Carolina), but they fought with the Native North Americans and their colony did not survive. Two years later, Raleigh made a second attempt to set up a colony, but this failed too.

This model of a settlers' ship is moored on the Roanoke River, where Raleigh founded his colony.

Food from America

Some adventurous merchants sailed to North and South America and brought back new foods such as potatoes, tomatoes, peppers and pineapples. Tobacco was also imported from the New World and it became fashionable for English gentlemen to smoke clay pipes.

Sir Walter Raleigh was greedy and ambitious. He hoped to use his American colony as a base from which to raid Spanish ships.

Science, medicine and technology

During the Tudor period, an exciting movement called the Renaissance swept through Europe. The Renaissance began in Italy in the 14th century and was inspired by the learning of the Ancient Greeks and Romans. It led people to examine the world around them and come up with new ideas.

This portrait by Hans Holbein, painted in 1533, shows two young men with a strong interest in science. One holds a telescope, while on the table between them are scientific instruments used in astronomy and for measuring time. At the base of the picture is a distorted skull, revealing the artist's interest in the science of optics (how people see things).

Caxton's printing press

In 1476 William Caxton set up the first English printing press. He copied his press from Johannes Gutenberg's famous invention, made in Germany in the 1450s. Printing presses could produce large quantities of books very quickly. This led to a rapid spread of knowledge across the world.

William Caxton printed over 100 books.

Alchemists or chemists?

The Tudors did not study science like we do today, but they did carry out experiments. Some experimenters, known as alchemists, hoped to turn metal into gold. Even though they failed, they learned how to make some chemicals and invented some scientific instruments.

Understanding anatomy

In the Middle Ages, the leaders of the Church had banned the dissection (cutting up) of human bodies. But Henry VIII allowed the bodies of four hanged criminals to be dissected each year. This was an important step towards a better understanding of human anatomy. Eventually it led to the improved treatment of diseases.

An alchemist's laboratory in 1590s

Artists, musicians and writers

The Tudor period was a great time for artists, musicians and writers. They were welcomed at court by King Henry VIII and Queen Elizabeth, and the English theatre flourished in Elizabeth's reign.

This delicate miniature of Queen Elizabeth was painted by Nicholas Hilliard. It was not much bigger than the picture on this page!

Portrait painting

All important people had their portraits painted. Kings and queens were shown in their finest robes, and merchants displayed their wealth and possessions. Artists also painted family portraits, showing parents and children and even pet dogs and birds! Some Tudor artists created exquisite miniature portraits. These were tiny paintings that could be carried in a pocket or a purse.

The painter Hans Holbein worked in the court of King Henry VIII. This Holbein portrait shows the King's son, Prince Edward, when he was just two years old.

Music and musicians

Wealthy Tudor boys and girls learned to play the lute, the harp or the virginals (an early keyboard instrument). Poorer people played the bagpipes, flutes and drums. Choirs sang religious anthems and small groups of singers performed madrigals. Some outstanding composers wrote for voices and instruments. The music of William Byrd and Thomas Tallis is still played and admired today.

King Henry VIII and Queen Elizabeth both loved to play the lute, and Henry was a talented composer.

Plays and poetry

William Shakespeare was the leading writer of the Tudor age. He wrote 38 plays and over a hundred poems. Christopher Marlowe and Ben Jonson wrote lively plays, and Sir Philip Sydney, Sir Walter Raleigh and Sir Edmund Spenser were brilliant poets. Spenser wrote a very long poem called *The Faerie Queene*, which he dedicated to Queen Elizabeth.

This is a modern performance of Shakespeare's play *The Tempest*. It is being staged in the Globe Theatre, which has been rebuilt to look as it did in the 1590s.

Facts and figures

Between 1500 and 1600 the number of people living in England doubled from two million to four million.

One in three people in Tudor England lived in poverty without enough food to eat. Nine out of ten died before they were 40.

As she grew older Queen Elizabeth wore a lot of make-up. She painted her lips with juice from berries and covered her face with a thick white paste. The paste was made from lead, which was later found to be poisonous.

The flushing toilet was invented by one of Queen Elizabeth's courtiers. Sir John Harrington made a 'water closet' with a set of levers that sent water from a tank into the toilet to flush it out.

The first potatoes arrived in England in Tudor times. They were brought by merchant ships from America. At first, potatoes were seen as an expensive luxury!

People in Tudor times tried to protect themselves from the plague by burning bunches of herbs. They believed that the smoke from the herbs would kill off the plague.

Some people deliberately coloured their teeth black to make themselves seem wealthy. It was known that sugar made your teeth go black, and only the very rich could afford to buy it!

Glossary

anatomy The structure of a body.

anthem A song sung by a choir.

astronomy The study of stars and planets.

burned at the stake Killed by being tied to a wooden stake and then burned to death.

cauldron A large metal cooking pot.

chamber pot A pot kept in a bedroom and used instead of a toilet.

colony A place that has been settled by people from another country and is controlled by that country.

courtier Someone who is close to the monarch and spends a lot of time at the royal court.

dedicate To write or produce something in honour of a person.

fleet A large group of ships.

flourish To grow and succeed.

gallows A wooden frame used for hanging criminals.

import To bring foreign goods into a country.

inherit To receive a title, money or property from someone.

jester An entertainer who tells jokes and performs comic dances.

lance A long spear used by a knight riding a horse.

loot To steal things, especially from ships or houses.

madrigal A song for a small group of singers, with parts for different voices.

navy The ships and sailors that fight for a country at sea.

persecute To treat cruelly and unfairly.

pestle and mortar A thick stick and a bowl, used for grinding spices and other things.

plague A serious disease which spreads quickly.

playwright Someone who writes plays.

Protestant A Christian who does not belong to the Roman Catholic Church.

reconstruction Something that has been made to look like something from the past.

Roman Catholic A Christian who belongs to the Church headed by the Pope in Rome.

spit A metal rod that has meat spiked on it. The spit is rotated over the fire to cook the meat.

stocks A wooden frame with holes in it, for locking up criminals.

stoke To add more fuel to a fire.

succeed To take over from someone in an important position or job.

tavern An inn or pub.

tournament A competition.

Further reading

In Tudor Times (Men, Women and Children), Jane Bingham (Wayland, 2011)

The Tudors (The Gruesome Truth About), Matt Buckingham (Wayland, 2012)

Tudors (Children in History), Fiona MacDonald (Watts, 2012)

The Tudors (Craft Topics), Rachel Wright (Watts, 2008)

The Tudors and Stuarts in Britain (Tracking Down), Liz Gogerly (Watts, 2013)

Websites

http://www.tudorbritain.org/
A site for children created by the Victoria and Albert Museum and The National Archives.
It includes tours and games, such as a Tudor tournament.

http://www.hrp.org.uk/PalaceKids/discover/allabouttudors
A fun site for children created by the Royal Palaces. It features videos, games and craft ideas.

http://www.bbc.co.uk/history/british/tudors/
A BBC website written by subject experts, with features on daily life, the age of exploration,
William Shakespeare and art and architecture. The site also has a children's sections, with games
and foul facts.

http://www.tudorhistory.org/
A large site on the Tudors, including sections on Henry's wives, Tudor buildings, and a guide to
who's who in Tudor times.

Index